Published by
Federation of Family History Societies (Publications) Ltd.
2-4 Kiler Street,
Ramsbottom, Bury,
Lancashire BL0 3BS,
United Kingdom

Copyright © Lilian Gibbens

ISBN 1 86006 102 8

First published 1997
Second edition 1999

Printed and bound by
Oxuniprint,
Great Clarendon Street,
Oxford OX2 6DP

Ba...
...
and
for Family Historians
SECOND EDITION
Lilian Gibbens

SERIES EDITOR
Pauline M. Litton

FEDERATION OF FAMILY HISTORY SOCIETIES

CONTENTS

Introduction	2
Death	2
Burial	3
Records of Death and Burial	6
Some Points to Remember	13
Useful Addresses	14
Bibliography	14

INTRODUCTION

Death is a consistent factor in human life. It is the common experience of every living thing. This guide deals with the several Death and Burial, and ancillary, records which the family historian may encounter during research; the type of record repository in which they can be found; some of the problems or pitfalls which may occur when using them; the various guides and indexes which can be utilised to locate records of death and burial; and books which supply more detailed information. An * indicates that more information can be found at the back of the booklet.

Check in advance of a visit whether the Register Office, Record Office, or library in question holds the records you wish to consult, whether you need to book a seat/microform reader in advance and whether microform or printed copies of the records are held in a repository which you can more conveniently visit. The Family History Library of the Church of Jesus Christ of Latter-day Saints (the Mormons) in Salt Lake City* holds microform copies of many of the records mentioned in this booklet; its worldwide Family History Centres will either hold microform copies of the records or be able to obtain them for you to read in return for a small charge.

Many family historians like to have copies of death and burial documents relating to their ancestors, for example, post-1837 civil registration certificates, parish register entries before this date, wills both before and after 12 January 1858 and obituaries etc. Much depends on whether the record repository which holds the records possesses a reader-printer as very few repositories now photocopy originals but many will, if equipment permits, take copies from microform. If they cannot oblige, try Salt Lake City*.

DEATH

When a person dies certain needs arise.
1. *To dispose of the body.* Not so urgent in these days of refrigeration, but very urgent in earlier times, especially so in the warmer months.
2. *To assuage the grief of the relatives* through the process of grieving, going through the ritual of the funeral, watching the interment, etc.
3. *To keep alive the memory of the deceased* through the creation of memorial books, the erection of memorial stones, etc.
4. *To dispose of the deceased person's goods and chattels and real estate* by means of the Will and Testament.

And sometimes

5. *To show other relatives, neighbours, friends and acquaintances that you are wealthier than they are or are not as poor as they thought you were* by the size of the funeral, the accoutrements, clothing, numbers attending and the lavishness of the reception or 'wake'.

The 'ritual of death' begins immediately after death. The next-of-kin must obtain a certificate, stating the cause of death, from a member of the medical profession, then register the death; the death certificate is then passed to the Undertaker (or Funeral Director) who (usually) makes all the arrangements for the disposal of the body, including notifying the local Registrar of the proposed place of burial or cremation. Not long ago, the local vicar would have helped with these arrangements. When death occurs by accident, or is sudden and unexpected, an Inquest on the body may be required before a death certificate is issued. If the deceased's family have no religious connections the undertaker will arrange for a priest (or a representative of the Humanist Society) to say the burial service. Disposal of the body may be by burial or, more commonly now, by cremation. Choice may be limited by the place in which the deceased lived: a churchyard burial is more likely in a rural parish than in an urban area.

The deceased's will may contain instructions for his/her funeral but legally the body is the possession of the executors and they may do with it what they will. Criticism may follow if those wishes are not observed but other factors may have an influence.

Changing Fashions

Our image of funerals is largely influenced by novelists, such as Charles Dickens. In some families (or communities) a funeral was something for which a poor man might beggar himself, struggling to pay insurance premiums to guarantee a sufficiently elaborate funeral that would not embarrass his family. A pauper's funeral implied disgrace! The last sixty years alone have brought changes. In the 1940s relatives and friends visited the deceased's home to pay their last respects. Often the front room or parlour was set aside for the purpose; the deceased rested in a coffin set upon the table; fires were extinguished, curtains drawn, mirrors covered in case the spirit of the dead person appeared in them, and clocks were stopped as a mark of respect. Everyone wore black for the funeral (and, in the case of close relatives, for a period of mourning after the funeral). If funds were short, a black arm-band could be worn, but the wearer incurred a degree of scorn or pity! During World War II clothing shortages, the 'rules' were relaxed and black arm-bands became common. Nowadays, the deceased 'rests' at the funeral parlour and funeral directors say that even viewing the body at their premises rarely happens.

BURIAL

Burial in the Middle Ages

In the Middle Ages the desire for a decent burial was more or less universal. Funerals were given a great deal of thought. Rich people were prepared to spend a lot of money on mourning clothes, torches, candles and the saying of masses for the dead; they gave money to the church, and the poor, to ensure the deceased person entered heaven. Nobles, or rich merchants, of the later Middle Ages chose interment within the church itself; beautifully carved memorials were erected, with figures of the deceased, together with stained-glass windows depicting family heraldry and that of families with which they intermarried. Poor people were buried in their parish churchyard. A description of what happened when a person died during mediaeval times is given by Christopher Daniell* in ***Death and Burial in Medieval England.***

A Place of Burial

From early modern times factors influencing the place of burial have been: the deceased's personal choice, the place of death, availability of space at a given location, cause of death, cost of burials at different locations, the personal status of the deceased or his/her close relatives, and a right to burial in a specific place; all interact, but some have greater impact than others.

The cause of death had very little effect on the place of burial, other than in cases of suicide, still births, and at times of epidemics. Suicides were forbidden burial in consecrated ground unless judged insane when they died. Occasionally, out of respect for the family, an incumbent would bury a suicide in ground on the north side of the church, but could not recite the burial service. Evidence suggests that churches were prepared to bury plague victims; in London, when the rate of mortality was very high (when the Black Death raged in the City of London from 1348 to 1350 and the Great Plague in 1665) bodies were placed into communal pits like those discovered in East Smithfield (Kaner*). Elsewhere the discovery of human bones in fields close to towns and villages suggests that those who died from the plague were buried in places other than the churchyard. Dead Man's Field, at Ealing in Middlesex, is a site where those who died of the plague were buried. Wealthy people were able to pay for burial in the chancel of a church or a churchyard mausoleum. Children, servants and apprentices were often buried in cheaper, less favoured locations. At certain times the holding of Puritan or nonconformist views, or an increase in population, influenced choice. Puritans frequently asked to be buried *'not in any church ... chapel or churchyard ... but in some barn, outhouse or field'.* The New Churchyard, situated outside Bishopsgate in London, was not attached to any of the City churches, although it was consecrated; it was used by those who wished to dissociate themselves from their parish church. Common Law gave an individual the right to be buried in the parish in which he died. Under Church Law an individual could be buried where he chose, providing his executors carried out his wishes. In practice, if a person was buried in a parish other than that in which he normally resided, the 'burying church' was obliged to pay over part of the income from the burial (which comprised offerings and fees) to the parish of the deceased; the exact proportion of income never was formally determined or written down. Some people elected (and still do elect) to be interred close to the grave of a relative, such as a wife, mother, father, or others, even if it meant transporting the body a considerable distance. On occasions the resting place is determined by sudden, unexpected death. A householder under whose roof a death took place had the duty to have the body taken to a grave decently covered; he was not obliged to send the body 'home'. Burials of babies, children, servants and married women were usually arranged by heads of households; evidence of this can be seen in burial register entries which identify servants, children and wives in relation to the master of the house, for example: 'Joan, the wife of Robert Smith' or 'Samuel, a child of Robert Smith' or 'Mary, maidservant at Robert Smith's house'.

Making Space

By the process of decay, a body buried in the ground eventually will take up less space than it did when first interred. In early times, unless the deceased was wealthy, the body was placed in the ground wrapped in a shroud. Soon, only the bones remain, easily moved to allow further burials. Placing the body in a wooden box (a coffin) slowed down the process of decay. In some churchyards and burial grounds, especially in urban areas, bodies were crowded into the earth. Such crowding-in meant that old graves had to be re-opened and bones disturbed more and more frequently. A few churches had Charnel Houses in which bones were stored; the crypts of many churches today were such 'bone houses'.

The Need for new Burial Grounds

As early as 1582 the Lord Mayor of London was complaining in a letter that it was scarcely possible to make a new grave in St Paul's Churchyard without corpses being laid open. Samuel Pepys recalls in his **Diary** the Sexton who said: '*for 6d I will jostle them together but will make room for him*'. The Bishop of London's Register for 1559–1621 records the consecration of new churchyards for seven City parishes — mostly after 1610; although some were replacements, others were additional grounds. Pressure on London burial grounds was eased a little in the late 1660s when London's population growth slowed down.

During the eighteenth and early nineteenth centuries parishes such as St George, Hanover Square, and St Martin in the Fields had to seek out space in which to bury their dead in suburban areas, like Camden and Bayswater, while the parish of St Bride's, Fleet Street, obtained land a mere few yards distant from the churchyard. Other densely inhabited towns and cities experienced similar problems as population expanded.

Private and Civil Cemeteries

Paul Joyce* states that 'before 1821 there were no proper public cemeteries at all in Great Britain' apart from early non-parochial burial grounds such as Bunhill Fields (London), which was established in 1665, Clifton Graveyard in Belfast (founded in 1774), the Calton Hill Cemetery in Edinburgh (which was in use by 1778) and the several old Jewish burial grounds, which were created in response to the needs of religious communities. Bunhill Fields was open to the deceased of all denominations but mostly was used by nonconformists. The Rosary, in Norwich, was probably the first nineteenth century cemetery (founded in 1821 by a dissenting minister in memory of his wife). Like Bunhill Fields, the Norwich Rosary permitted the burial of Anglicans as well as nonconformists. In Liverpool, in 1825, the Necropolis Cemetery was opened to nonconformists and in 1825 the St James Cemetery was begun. The first cemeteries not entirely related to any church or chapel were opened as private ventures. In London, for example, a Scots landscape gardener, John Claudius Loudon (1783–1843), published proposals for a series of cemeteries to surround London, to be laid out as 'botanical gardens' for the 'pleasure and instruction of visitors'. Loudon's proposals influenced the establishment of the General Cemetery Company in 1830, which opened Kensal Green Cemetery in 1831. Encouraged by the financial success of Kensal Green other cemetery companies were formed and Norwood Cemetery (1836), Highgate Cemetery (1836), Brompton (1838), Abney Park and Nunhead (both in 1839), and Tower Hamlets (1840) all came into use. Later, in 1852 for London, and

1853 for the remainder of the country, Acts of Parliament enabled local authorities to purchase and use land for the purpose of burial; it is at this time that many civil cemeteries came into existence and burials ceased in urban churchyards.

Burial Fees etc.

In mediaeval times the Church, and its priests, derived income from the ritual of burial, by way of mortuary fees, fees for commemorative services, grave digging, bell ringing and the use of the parish coffin, hearse or hearse cloth. The Church claimed it did not charge for these *services* but for the *time* devoted to them. A graduated scale of burial fees (agreed by the Vestry and approved by the Diocesan Chancellor) was used at each churchyard, varying according to the more or less desirable areas in the churchyard or the church itself. After the Reformation burial rites still carried fees payable to the Church but some rituals were eliminated; fees were payable both to the parish Churchwardens and to the Sexton; the cost of burial included the 'customary duty' for 'breaking ground' payable to the Churchwarden, and a fee for digging the grave, which was given to the Sexton. Reduced fees were charged for the burial of children.

Modern Parochial Fees

Currently, the Church Commissioners agree the fees payable by law, publishing a *Table of Parochial Fees* on 1 January each year. Charges are made for funeral services held in churches, cemeteries or crematoria; for a churchyard burial immediately after a service in church; for an extra fee a person can be buried in a churchyard on a different day to the service. The burial of still-born infants or those who die within one year after birth is free. Burials in cemeteries (and cremations) also incur charges; as a rule all these fees are incorporated into the fees charged by the Funeral Director.

How soon after Death did Burial take Place?

Stephen Porter's study of death and burial* in the parish of St Mary Woolnoth, in the City of London, during the period 1653–1699 suggests a predominance of burials occurred within a maximum of 72 hours after death; he compared his London figures with data from research relating to seventeenth century Oxford* and a group of six Yorkshire parishes over the period 1647–1666. The need for quick burial is obvious, especially among the poor unable to preserve the body. Rich people could buy costly embalming of a body, have it wrapped in waxed or tarred sheets and placed in a lead-lined double coffin if the body had to be carried some distance. Ordinary people made do with a plain wooden coffin, or merely a shroud. Generally, nineteenth century burials seem to have taken place about one week after death, as they do today. Cemetery records may supply both date of burial and of death, or the date of registration of death, as in the burial record of Sarah Wilkinson (aged 96) of Lower Edmonton in Middlesex, who died on 1 August 1853 and was interred at the Burial Ground at St Thomas Square, Mare Street in Hackney on 8 August.

When did Burials take Place?

Evidence suggests burials took place every day of the week, even on Christmas and Easter Days. Changing seasons seem to have had little effect; other data indicate a small increase in the number of child burials in warmer weather in cities (perhaps due to deaths resulting from consuming 'spoiled' food); but, more old people than young died in the winter time. In *The Victorian Undertaker*, Trevor May states the death rate of infants under one year old to be more or less constant at around 153 for every thousand live births in the closing decades of the nineteenth century; today the figure is under sixteen per thousand. In exceptionally cold winters the numbers of deaths increased in some rural areas, maybe from the effects of the weather but, more likely, due to starvation at a time when food becomes scarce. Frost and snow delayed burials due to the impossibility of digging graves in the hard, frozen ground; in such conditions bodies were often stockpiled! Even when people died in circumstances requiring an inquest burial usually took place within 72 hours of death.

Trades' Guilds and City of London Livery Companies

Trades' Guilds and Livery Companies arranged their members' funerals; all members were expected to attend each funeral, the day and time set out on tickets (with illustrations of funerals).

Funeral Fashions and Rituals

The way in which funerals were conducted, styles of mourning clothes and shrouds and coffin design, can be ascertained from illustrations on livery tickets, memorial cards, trade cards and Bills of Mortality, as well as sculptures and bas-reliefs on monuments in churches and churchyards.

Pall Bearers

The Pall was a cloth draped over the coffin as it was carried to church. Pall-bearers were men or women who supported (held) the hem of the pall and walked beside the coffin as it was borne through the streets and into church. A married man's pall was supported by his married friends; that of a single man by his bachelor friends; and those of children, married women or widows by male relatives or the undertaker's men. A spinster's pall was held by women (Litten*).

Who made coffins?

Until the emergence of Undertakers, coffins were generally made by carpenters, cabinet makers, or anyone skilled with wood.

The first Undertakers

Undertaking began in the 1640s. Advertising materials (printed Trade cards, early directories, pattern books, bill heads), contemporary written accounts, and livery company admission books, give an idea of the trade. Collections of trades' cards are held in archives, libraries and museums. Ambrose Heal's two books* provide an illustrated ready reference. William Boyce, the first recorded person trading as an undertaker, opened a shop in about 1675, closely followed by William Russell, painter and coffin maker of London; in 1689 Russell agreed with the College of Arms that, for a fee, College members would attend all funerals arranged by him.

Early Undertakers

A hierarchy evolved in the undertaking world: (i) Coffin Makers: who may have performed funerals occasionally in addition to making coffins; (ii) Undertakers: coffin makers regularly performing funerals (in some places, an undertaker dealt only with parish funerals and was himself very poor); (iii) Funeral Furnishers: who bought in ready-made coffins, dressed them to their clients' wishes, provided accessories and performed funerals. By the end of the nineteenth century the three separate trades had amalgamated to become Funeral Directors.

Victorian Undertakers

By 1843 the trade was well-established. Edwin Chadwick, the journalist and reformer, quoted Mr Dix, a successful London undertaker performing an average of 800 funerals a year: *'I frequently perform funerals three deep; that is, I do it for one person, who does it for another, who does it for the relatives of the deceased, he being the first person applied to. People generally apply to the nearest person. Everybody calls himself an undertaker. The numerous men employed as bearers become undertakers, although they have never done anything until they have got the job. I have known one of these men get a new suit of clothes out of a funeral of one decent mechanic.'*

Specialist manufacturers produced goods for the undertaking trade: coffins and fabric covered outer cases, coffin furniture (metal fittings on coffins), and other accoutrements. Larger undertakers hired out the stocks-in-trade to smaller undertakers who, in turn, hired them out to the public: items such as velvet palls, room hangings, candlesticks, sconces, feathers, gloves and cloaks. In London these manufactories were situated in Southwark and Whitechapel, both close to docks, foundries and timberyards. Spitalfields was the centre of the 'Black Stuff' industry, producing rich, embroidered silks and velvets for distribution to the funeral trade throughout the country. Black silk was produced in Essex, Hertfordshire and at silk mills throughout England and Wales, but its quality did not surpass that made by the Spitalfields weavers.

RECORDS OF DEATH AND BURIAL

Civil Registration

This is not the place to discuss the system of Civil Registration — introduced in 1837 in

England and Wales, 1855 in Scotland, 1864 in Ireland, 1840 in Guernsey, 1842 in Jersey and 1878 (for deaths) in the Isle of Man. The indexes to registered deaths for England and Wales can be consulted at the Office for National Statistics (ONS) at the Family Records Centre (FRC)* in Myddelton Street, Islington. Death Certificates can be purchased in person, or by post. Those visiting the FRC for the first time may wish to read Audrey Collins' *Basic Facts About Using the Family Records Centre* * before making the trip. Read Tom Wood's *An Introduction to Civil Registration* * to find out how to locate and order certificates from the several General Registrars' Offices. Certificates in England, Wales and Ireland all provide the same information: when and where died, name and surname, sex, age, occupation, cause of death, signature and description and residence of the informant, date when registered and the signature of the registrar. Date of birth replaces age from 1969.

Scottish death certificates are the most informative of all the separate British death certificates. Depending upon the date, they may show the full names of the deceased person; their sex, and age; the date, time and place of death; the occupation of the deceased; their marital status, which may include the name of any spouse or former spouse; the birth place of the deceased; full names and ages of children and whether alive or dead and the name of the informant, and the date of birth of the deceased from 1967. Scottish death certificates may be obtained from New Register House in Edinburgh. The Statutory Index to Scottish deaths from 1855 to date can also be used in London via *Scot Link* at the Family Records Centre. The fee to use this service is £4.00 per half hour or less, £8.00 per hour up to a maximum of two hours. You must book to use this service either in person at the FRC or by telephone (0171 533 6438).

Civil registration was introduced into Ireland in 1845 when all non-Roman Catholic marriages were required to be registered. In 1864, the existing poor law unions (PLUs) were divided into registration districts and all births, marriages and deaths had to be registered. Civil Registration records and indexes for the whole of Ireland up to 1921 and for the Republic of Ireland (Eire) from 1922 are held at the General Register Office (GRO) in Dublin. Those relating to Northern Ireland from 1922 are held at the General Register Office of Northern Ireland, Belfast (GRONI). For further details you may like to read Bill Davis' two booklets *An Introduction to Irish Research* * and *Basic Facts About Irish Family History Research* *.

Parish Registers of the Anglican Church

Many early burial registers date from about 1598 but may contain copy-entries going back to 1538. Burial entries may be written among those for baptisms and marriages; such 'mixed' registers may be catalogued as 'Composite Registers'. Sometimes a register will be divided into three separate sections: baptisms at the front, marriages in the middle and burials at the back. Later separate volumes were used for the three events. Generally, burials were recorded more conscientiously than baptisms, but less so than marriages. Read *An Introduction to Church Registers* * by Lilian Gibbens for details of the ecclesiastical and civil laws relating to the keeping of these documents.

Whose Burials will be Recorded?

Burial entries rarely identify the deceased precisely. Some incumbents only registered burials by Anglican rites, excluding suicides, excommunicates, executed criminals and unbaptised children; burials of still-born children were rarely recorded. Some Roman Catholics and Dissenters were buried privately, sometimes at night, in the churchyard, with the incumbent 'turning a blind eye'. Entries for Roman Catholics and other dissenters are not common; an example is the entry in the registers of Christchurch, Hampshire for 14 April 1604: *'Christian Steevens, the wife of Thomas Steevens, died in Childbirth and was buried by women for she was a papishe'.* Generally bodies of recusants, baptists, quakers etc. were treated with scant respect by the Anglican clergy, as reflected by the entry at Warleggan, Cornwall, 1681: *'George Piper, an Anabaptist, tumbled in ye ground Feb 25'.* It was the duty of an Anglican clergyman not to read the burial service over the body of a person who had not been baptised by the Anglican rite; he could refuse Christian burial to any whose baptism was doubtful. It is probable, however, that most dissenters buried in parish churchyards were not singled out for special attention in the register, evidence of nonconformity being culled from other evidence.

Reasons why a Burial may not be Recorded in an Anglican Register

Some omissions may be for reasons similar to those stated in the register of Egglescliffe, Durham: *'1644, In this year there died of the plauge[sic] in this towne, one and twenty people: they are not all buried in the churchyard, and are not in the register'.* The Abstract of the Population Returns for 1801 mentions that Anglican burial registers do not include details of the following:

1. Dissenters who belong to Congregations in towns who have their own burial ground, as well as the Jews and Roman Catholics in London (such cemeteries being opened after the Toleration Act of 1689).
2. Those persons who, from reasons of poverty or convenience, bury their dead without ceremony.
3. Those children who died before baptism, and therefore are not registered, and have no ceremony.
4. Errors which occur in small parishes where the minister is not resident.
5. Those individuals in the Army and Navy who die abroad.

Other omissions may result from the loss of pages from a register (or the loss of a entire register) or the failure to record events at times of political or religious unrest. Occasionally registers are taken away by a church official, such as an Archdeacon, and never returned. The minister at Kingsdown in Kent recorded in his register in 1814, the burial of: *'Phillips, Clerk of the Parish 19 years. A respectable man & an excellent reader. The man who burnt the old Parish Registers'.*

Genealogical Information in Burial Registers prior to 1813

Early burial entries are very brief, for example: '5th May 1588, Mary Smith'. The addition of a father's name *may* indicate a child: '5th May 1588, Mary Smith a daughter of Francis Smith'; however, the entry may refer to a middle-aged spinster living alone or with her father. If a child is baptised with the same name as his father, and there is a burial record for someone of the same name within a year of baptism, then it is *probably* the child, not the father, who died. Deceased persons of social standing may be indicated by a title or description, such as Master (Mr), Mistress (Mrs), Dame, Gentleman (Gent), Armiger (Arm), Esquire (Esq) and Yeoman (Yeo). Register entries may also state the location of the burial, for example, 'in the chancel', 'by the altar' or 'in the churchyard' or the place is indicated by abbreviations to which no key exists today. The burial register of Cranbrook in Kent illustrates the varying amounts of information that may be contained in such volumes:

1610, June 1	Houldon, Thomas
1616, Sept 16	Houldon, a crisomer of John
1621, Nov 25	Houlden Mary, a child
1651, June 1	Kinge, Mary Holdman, daughter of Jeremiah Holdman and wife of John Kinge, butcher
1657, Oct 12	Holden, Sam: son of Mr Richard of Brenden, clothier and of Frances Hodges, uxor
1701, March 6	John son of Robt Holden of Hawkridge, gent
1724, Sept 3	James Stone, yeoman, Quaker

Burial Records during the Interregnum (1649–1660)

The Commonwealth decreed that burials be recorded in a 'fair vellum book' and the death date noted. Few parishes appear to have complied. In September 1653 custody of burial registers (and those of marriage and births) was removed from the incumbent and passed to the 'Parish Register' who was elected by the parish ratepayers. Occasionally, registers from this period contain extra information, as at Edwinstowe, Nottinghamshire: *'8 March 1653/4: Anne wife of Thos. Hallam deceased. Was my first Master's wife which taught me to spell and read in my childhood'.*

Dade Registers and Barrington Registers

Dade burial registers may provide the following information: the Christian name and surname of the deceased; descent; profession; date of death and where buried; cause of death and age. Their format was the idea of William Dade, a York clergyman, and was adopted by Archbishop Markham of York in 1777, who tried to enforce their use in the parishes in the Diocese of York. Brief details of extant Dade registers in Yorkshire, Lancashire, Nottinghamshire (once in the Diocese of York), and a few elsewhere are given in the two articles cited in the Bibliography. The Rev. Shute Barrington, Bishop of Durham (formerly Bishop of Salisbury) instigated the use of slightly simpler registers in Wiltshire, Bristol, Berkshire and Durham. Some registers have been transcribed: for example, those in Berkshire have been transcribed by Rosemary Church of Wiltshire FHS. Use of these registers virtually ceased in 1812.

Burials in Woollen

Acts of Parliament were passed in 1666 and 1678 to encourage the wool trade by ordering that corpses were to be wrapped in wool only. A deceased's relatives had to swear an affidavit (a written statement made on oath) before a Justice of the Peace (or a clergyman) within eight days of the funeral, declaring that they had complied with the terms of the law. Sometimes at the close of the burial service the clergyman would ask: 'Who makes the Affidavit?'. A satisfactory reply was indicated in the burial register by the word 'Affidavit' or an abbreviation of that word. A £5 penalty was imposed on the estate of every person not buried in woollen, on the householder in whose house he died, on the person(s) connected with the funeral, on the minister failing to certify the non-receipt of the affidavits and on any overseers neglecting to levy the penalty. Half of each fine was given to the poor, the other half to the informer. It was not unknown for a family member to play the part of informer (especially in well-off families) and so reduce the penalty to £2.10s. The record of burial of Elizabeth Wilkinson, in Aldborough, Yorkshire hints at such collusion: *'The Information of Margaret Robinson made on Oath before Mr Thomas Wilkinson, her grand child that she, the said Mrs Eliz. Wilkinson was buryed in Linning on the fifth day of Feb: 1717 contrary to the Act of Parliament for bureying in woolen'.* Thomas Wilkinson of Boroughbridge Hall was the local JP (Tate*).

Taxes on Burials

In 1694 a duty of 4s (four shillings) was imposed on burials of all non-paupers; the Stamp Act of 1782 granted a duty of 3d (three pence) on all register entries of burial. Details of payment of duties will not often be found. For further information see: *Introduction to Church Registers*.*

Burials from 1813

George Rose's Act of 1812 came into force on 1 January 1813: it required all burials to be entered in a separate book, with the information set out under the printed headings: name of deceased, abode, age, date of burial and the name of the officiating minister.

Bishops' Transcripts (BTs)

The BTs (or Bills of Register) were supposed to be copies of the parish register entries made annually on Lady Day (25 March), setting out all the entries made during the previous year; however, information on the transcripts may differ from that provided in the registers and both sources should be consulted. These records are now held in English Diocesan Record Offices or the National Library of Wales; see the relevant *Gibson Guide*.* for details of location and availability. There are no BTs for Scotland or Ireland.

Pauper Burials

Right to burial at parish expense was given only by settlement. Such burials may be indicated by the word 'pauper' or the letter 'P' set against the entry. A body conveyed from the parish where death occurred may also be indicated, as at Appledore in Kent: *'1722, 2 July: Elizabeth Bishops, brought from Great Chart to this parish'.* Many paupers were buried in common or communal graves (especially so in the North of England). Burial from a workhouse may be noted in parish registers; sometimes separate sections at the end of a year's entries may be used to do so. Pre-1834 workhouses may have kept registers of deaths and burials and these will be held in County Record Offices or local archives. See *Poor Law Union Records, Parts 1–3*,* by

J.S.W. Gibson et al. for details of extant post-1834 Union Workhouse registers of deaths and burials.

The Location of Anglican Burial Registers

Anglican burial registers will be in the custody of a designated diocesan repository, usually the County Record Office. In London records are held at Guildhall Library* and the London Metropolitan Archives*. The University Libraries of York (Borthwick Institute of Historical Research) and Durham also hold a great number of registers for their counties. Generally, microform copies are provided for public access. Copies of these may be available at local archives, at the Family History Centres run by the LDS Church* (the Mormons), or in Salt Lake City. A list of Family History Centres in England and Wales can be obtained from the GSU, UK (see page 14 for the address). For details relating to record offices see the relevant *Gibson Guide** or Joy Wade Moulton's guide*. Another useful book is the *Atlas and Index of Parish Registers**, 2nd edition, by Cecil Humphery-Smith. For information specific to Greater London consult *London Local Archives: A Directory of Local Authority Record Offices and Libraries*, published jointly by Guildhall Library and the Greater London Archive Network (1994).

Nonconformist Burials and Burial Registers

Deaths are occasionally recorded in early nonconformist registers; before 1644 English nonconformist congregations did not keep registers as written material could be used against them by their persecutors. The first nonconformist denomination to keep registers regularly was the Society of Friends (known as the Quakers). Quakers do not have ministers who perform burials, but George Fox organised a system of registering family events that matched the terms of the 1653 Act relating to the keeping of registers by the 'Parish Register'. Quaker burials took place in parish churchyards, in gardens or in orchards, until their own burial grounds were established. The Monthly Meeting that covered the place *where the deceased was buried* had the responsibility for producing the burial note but this responsibility diminished with the advent of public cemeteries. Quaker burials are also listed in the Digest Registers produced by the Society of Friends in 1840–1842. For fuller details see the relevant volume in the series *My Ancestors Were . . .**. Copies of the Digest Registers are held centrally in Friends' House Library in Euston Road, London, as well as locally. See also Michael Gandy's *Basic Facts About English Nonconformity for Family Historians**.

In the eighteenth century, nonconformist meeting houses of all denominations increasingly began to have their own burial grounds, sometimes because of the refusal by the Anglican clergy to read the burial service over dissenters. Burial inside a chapel was uncommon. Records of interments in chapelyards are rarely found in parish registers; although legally obliged to, most nonconformist ministers did not send lists of burials to their Anglican counterparts. Nineteenth century nonconformists campaigned for the right of their own ministers to perform and register burials in parish churchyards, but this was not achieved until 1880.

Location of pre-1837 Nonconformist Registers

The Non-Parochial Registers Act of 1840 required all nonconforming congregations, including foreign and Roman Catholic Churches, to deposit their registers (or copies thereof) with the Registrar-General. A second deposit was organised in 1857 and a revised, consolidated list of all the registers in the custody of the General Register Office was published in 1859. Presently, the Public Record Office (PRO)* has custody of these documents, and microfilm copies are available for consultation at the Family Records Centre* and at many County Record Offices and libraries. The records of Bunhill Fields burial ground, in London, were also deposited in 1837; indexes to these are held at FRC and Guildhall Library, London. Individuals with origins in all parts of the UK are buried in Bunhill Fields. However, many nonconformist burials are recorded in Minute Books, which were not deposited with the Registrar-General. The locations of burial registers of the various denominations are given in the several books about nonconformists in the *My Ancestors Were...* series*, published by the Society of Genealogists (see Bibliography).

Location of post-1837 Nonconformist Registers

After 1837 most nonconformists were buried in public cemeteries and registered there. In rural areas burial may have taken place in parish churchyards, with the service taken by a nonconformist minister and the burial registered by the Anglican priest. The Registration of Burials Act, 1864, enforced the keeping of proper Registers of Burials for all burial grounds attached to nonconformist places of worship; copies had to be made and forwarded to Diocesan Registries, but register keeping ceased as public cemeteries were opened. Burial records may be held in 'circuit' or 'district' archives or in county record offices or local archives.

Roman Catholic Burials

Records of interments of Roman Catholics may be found in Anglican registers; few Roman Catholic churches had their own burial grounds before the nineteenth century. Churches without burial grounds may have recorded the names of members of the congregation buried in the Anglican churchyard. A small number of Roman Catholic registers were surrendered to the Registrar-General, but many were retained by individual churches. A number have been transcribed and published by the Catholic Record Society*. Some family history societies have also transcribed/indexed some registers. Generally, Catholic churches did not keep burial registers but registers of other events may contain notes of deaths or a record of a mass. See Michael Gandy's *Basic facts About Tracing Your Catholic Ancestry in England*. Sections of public cemeteries may be set aside for Roman Catholic burials. Notices of deaths appear in some early editions of the *Catholic Directory*.

Jewish Burial Grounds and Burial Registers

Information about burial registers kept by Jewish communities can be found in *National Index of Parish Registers, Vol. 3. Sources for Roman Catholic and Jewish Genealogy and Family History*, by D.J. Steel and E.R. Samuel (published by Society of Genealogists). See also *My Ancestors were Jewish*. If a burial ground is still in use, information may be had from the Cemetery Superintendent; if the ground is no longer used, it may be possible to visit by arrangement. Jewish registers were not surrendered to the Registrar-General in the 1840s; many are still held by individual synagogues, burial societies or cemeteries.

Before 1855 — Old Parish Registers (OPRs) in Scotland

The OPRs in Scotland are in the custody of the Registrar-General and can be consulted at New Register House in Edinburgh*. *Scot Link* at FRC does *not* provide any index to deaths before 1854. Very few Scottish parishes have burial registers. The records of burial were kept by people who ran the graveyards; once the responsibility of the church, but later the lot of those maintaining the graveyards. As a result some record entries may be sparse or non-existent and other records, such as accounts of persons borrowing the mort-cloth used in the ceremony, may have to be consulted. Gravestones may provide more information than written records. Also at the GRO in Scotland is the Register of Neglected Entries (1801–1854) which is a record of births, marriages and deaths proved to have occurred in Scotland between those dates, but not entered in the parish registers. Probate records are at the Scottish R.O., General Register House, Edinburgh EH1 3YY.

Registers of Burial in Eire and Northern Ireland

There are few, if any, Roman Catholic burial registers. A large number of the Church of Ireland registers were destroyed in 1922. It is suggested that readers who wish to trace parish records in Ireland should first read Chapter 3 'Parish Records' in *Tracing your Irish Ancestors*, by John Grenham*.

Pre-1837 Public Cemetery Records

The burial registers of some cemeteries established before 1837 are held at the Public Record Office, Ruskin Avenue, Kew; others may be held at county record offices or by local cemetery authorities.

Post-1837 Cemetery Records

The Superintendent's office at the cemetery or

crematorium may house the burial registers (or cremation registers) and lists of grave-lots. Private-grave registers may record who was buried in each plot, cost of the plot and each burial within it. Details of cemeteries can be found in local telephone books, under the relevant council and then Leisure and Amenities or Parks and Recreation. Always telephone or write before making a visit, to ascertain the whereabouts of the records (some cemeteries have closed and the records may have been transferred to another cemetery for safe keeping, to the Town Hall or Civic Centre, or a local record office). Before making, or requesting, a search in cemetery records it is necessary to know the date of death/burial, as few records are indexed. If the records are available for personal searches, a fee may not be charged; however, be prepared for a fee to be exacted if you request a search to be made by post. Charges range from £5 per single entry to £25 per year. There are multifarious websites relating to cemeteries on the Internet. However, readers should be aware that many of these sites are not the official websites of the cemeteries, even if they give the impression of being so; sometimes the data supplied are incorrect.

Family History Societies (FHS) — Burial Indexes

A number of family history societies have transcribed and/or indexed burial registers, BTs, cemetery registers or memorial inscriptions and have published them in book form or in microform. Some family history societies have produced lists of cemeteries in their area. A comprehensive list of family history societies who are members of the Federation of FHSs can be obtained from the Administrator*. See *Specialist Indexes for Family Historians* by J.S.W. Gibson and Elizabeth Hampson (FFHS). At the present time member societies of the FFHS are in the process of compiling a National Burials Index (computer database format).

Monumental Inscriptions (MIs)

Many FHSs have undertaken the recording of inscriptions on tombstones (gravestones) in churchyards and older cemeteries. Copies of the transcripts may have been deposited in local record offices, libraries, the Library of the Society of Genealogists (who have a large collection) and the Family History Library in Salt Lake City. Older transcripts, often produced by local Record Societies, may have been published. In Ireland, some Heritage and Research Centres, and some family history societies, have indexed the MIs in their areas. See *A Guide to Irish Churches and Graveyards* by B Mitchell* and *Sources for Irish Genealogy in the Library of the Society of Genealogists* compiled by Anthony Camp. Published local histories may also have quite large sections devoted to memorial inscriptions in the parish church.

Wills

Indexes to registered wills since 1858 are held at the Principal Registry of the Family Division, Probate Department, First Avenue House, 42—49 High Holborn, London WC1V 6NP (tel: 0171 936 7000) in Central London. If you are contemplating a first visit to First Avenue House you may wish to read Audrey Collins' *Basic Facts About Using Wills after 1858 and First Avenue House* *. If you are unable to visit First Avenue House then you can order wills by post by writing to The Postal Searches and Copies Department, The Probate Registry, Duncombe Place, York YO1 2EA (tel/fax: 01904 624210). Registered copies of wills proved at district registries are now often held by local record offices. Before 1858 probate was handled by ecclesiastical courts. Records of the Prerogative Court of Canterbury (PCC) are available for consultation on microform at the PRO Family Records Centre in Islington*; those of the Prerogative Court of York (PCY) are in the custody of the Borthwick Institute*. For information relating to wills read *An Introduction to Affection Defying the Power of Death: Wills, Probate and Death Duty Records*, by Jane Cox* and consult *Probate Jurisdictions: Where to Look for Wills*, compiled by Jeremy Gibson*.

Society of Genealogists

A list of parish register copies, including burial registers, at the Society of Genealogists, is published as *Parish Register Copies in the Library of the Society of Genealogists.* Nonconformist register copies in the Society of Genealogists are listed in the relevant volumes in the *My Ancestors were...* series.

Coroners' Records

A coroner has the duty to investigate the circumstances of unnatural, sudden or suspicious deaths, and deaths in prison. For a brief history, description and the location of these records see: Hunnisett (mentioned below) and *Coroners' Records in England and Wales** by Jeremy Gibson and Colin Rogers. Such records are only open to the public after 75 years. They may be found in the PRO and county record offices. Coroners' Inquisitions (Inquests) provide full details of a case, giving a complete social aspect of the family involved and details of witnesses; Coroners' Bills and Expenses provide only brief details (just sufficient information written down in order to allow the coroner to claim his expenses). Some Coroners' records have been transcribed and published; examples are the nineteenth century Full Inquisitions for Marlborough, Wiltshire, the Wiltshire County Coroners' Bills (transcribed by Jean Cole); eighteenth century Wiltshire Coroners' records (transcribed by Dr R.F. Hunnisett for Wiltshire Record Society) and *Sussex Coroners' Inquests 1558–1603* (transcribed by Dr Hunnisett, published by PRO, 1996). See also *My Ancestors were Freemen of the City of London** for details of inquests for the City of London and the ancient borough of Southwark. Many Coroners' records are lost or not open to public scrutiny and the only source of information may be newspaper reports of inquests.

Manorial Records

The deaths of copyhold tenants may be recorded in Court Books with extracts from the will of the deceased; particularly useful for periods when parish records are lacking or for the nineteenth century when many people became nonconformist and are not recorded in parish records.

Newspapers and Journals: Deaths, Obituaries and Inquests

Deaths notices in nineteenth-century local newspapers were not general before the 1870s. Obituaries, funerals of notable local residents, accidental deaths (usually particularly gruesome ones), murders and some suicides were occasionally reported, as well as Inquests relating to 'ordinary' people. *The Times* is a good source for deaths, burials and obituaries; also *Gentleman's Magazine, The Annual Register, Notes & Queries,* specialist professional journals and 'county' journals. See also the 'year books' of universities, colleges and 'institutes'. Annual 'magazines' produced by the 'old boys'/'old girls' societies of schools may feature detailed obituaries of deceased members (often written by close friends who had known the deceased for very many years).

Undertakers' Records

Relatively few undertakers' records have survived. Some long-established firms still retain their records, with those of businesses they have absorbed over the years; a few are deposited in CROs and local archive departments. It may be possible to trace the whereabouts of the records using the published guide produced by the Business Archives Council, which should be available in all reference libraries.

Commonwealth War Graves Commission

Under a Royal Charter of 1917, the Commonwealth War Graves Commission* was given the task of maintaining records of all those who died whilst serving with Commonwealth forces during World War I and World War II. The records are held on a database at the Head Office in Maidenhead. Details of the location of a grave or of a name can be provided free of charge to relatives of the deceased serviceman or, for a small fee, to other researchers. The facility, known as the Debt of Honour Register, can be accessed by the Internet (www.cwgc.org). The Civilian War Dead Roll of Honour contains 66,375 names of those who died during hostilities in World War II. The roll is contained in seven volumes and is kept near St George's Chapel in Westminster Abbey. Some of the cemetery and memorial registers maintained by the CWGC are available from them as publications. They also publish information sheets.

SOME POINTS TO REMEMBER

- The ages stated on death certificates and

- burial records are not necessarily accurate as they are usually provided by someone other than the deceased.
- In early documents the spelling of a name may not always be as expected; always check for name-variants.
- Social up-grading was common on death certificates — many agricultural labourers were described as farmers or solicitors' clerks omitted the clerk!
- People do not always die at home — the place of death stated on a death certificate may be the home of a relative, a house in which the deceased was a visitor, a hotel or boarding house, or a hospital.

USEFUL ADDRESSES

Federation of Family History Societies (FFHS)
Administrator: c/o The Benson Room, Birmingham & Midland Institute, Margaret Street, Birmingham B3 3BS
Publications: 2–4 Killer Street, Ramsbottom, Bury, Lancs BL0 9BZ

The main General Register Offices (for Civil Registration Records)
England & Wales: The Family Records Centre, 1 Myddelton Street, London EC1R 1UW

Postal applications for certificates
ONS, General Register Office, Postal Applications Section, Smedley Hydro, Trafalgar Road, Birkdale, Southport, Merseyside PR8 4HL

Scotland: New Register House, Edinburgh EH1 3YT

Republic of Ireland: GRO, Joyce House, 8–11 Lombard Street East, Dublin 2

Northern Ireland (post-1922 only): GRONI, Oxford House, 49–55 Chichester Street, Belfast BT1 4HR

Irish Genealogical Research Society: 82 Eaton Square, London SW1 9AJ

Church of Jesus Christ of Latter-day Saints: Genealogical Society of Utah, Family History Library, 35 North West Temple, Salt Lake City, Utah 84150 USA (enclose 3 IRCs or dollar bill)

GSU, UK: 185–187 Penns Lane, Sutton Coldfield, Birmingham, West Midlands B76 1JU (for the location of Family History Centres, *not* research queries)

Society of Genealogists: 14 Charterhouse Buildings, Goswell Road, London EC1M 7BA

Institute of Heraldic & Genealogical Studies: Northgate, Canterbury, Kent CT1 1BA (for Achievements, Parish Maps and Phillimore's Atlas)

Family Tree Magazine: 61 Great Whyte, Ramsey, Huntingdon, Cambs PE17 1HL

Guildhall Library: Aldermanbury, London EC2P 2EJ

Principal Registry of the Family Division (PPR): Probate Dept., First Avenue House, 42–49 High Holborn, London WC1V 6NP (tel: 0171 936 7000)
Postal applications to: PPR, Postal Searches and Copies Dept., The Probate Registry, Duncombe Place, York YO1 2EA (tel/fax: 01904 624210)

PRO: London Research Centre: Family Records Centre, 1 Myddelton Street, Islington EC1R 1UW

Catholic Central Library: Lancing Street, London NW1 1ND

Catholic Family History Society: 45 Gates Green Road, West Wickham, Kent BR4 9DE

Catholic Record Society: 114 Mount Street, London W1X 6AX

Religious Society of Friends: Friends' House, Euston Road, London NW1 2BJ

London Metropolitan Archives: 40 Northampton Road, London EC1R 0HB

Borthwick Institute of Historical Research: St Anthony's Hall, Peasholme Green, York YO1 2PW

Commonwealth War Graves Commission: 2 Marlow Road, Maidenhead, Berks. SL6 7DX (tel: 01628 634221)

BIBLIOGRAPHY

Aldous, Vivienne E., *My Ancestors were Freemen of the City of London,* Society of Genealogists, 1999.

Bellingham, Roger A., 'Dade Parish Registers', in *Family History News & Digest,* Vol. 10, No. 2, Sept. 1995 (FFHS).

Breed, G.R., *My Ancestors were Baptists,* Society of Genealogists, 1986, 3rd edition, 1995.

Camp Anthony J., *Sources for Irish*

Genealogy in the Library of the Society of Genealogists, Society of Genealogists, 2nd edition, 1998.

de Carteret, M., 'Strangers' Cemetery – St Peter Port, Guernsey', in *Devon Family Historian,* No. 71, Aug. 1994.

Clifford D.J.H., *My Ancestors were Congregationalists in England and Wales,* with a list of registers, Society of Genealogists, 1992.

Collins, Audrey, *Basic Facts About Using Wills after 1858 and First Avenue House,* FFHS, 1998.

Collins, Audrey, *Basic Facts About Using the Family Records Centre,* FFHS, 1997.

Cox, Jane, *An Introduction to Affection Defying the Power of Death: Wills, Probate & Death Duty Records,* FFHS, 1993.

Daniell, Christopher, *Death and Burial in Medieval England 1066–1550,* Routledge, London, 1997.

Davis, Bill, *Basic Facts About Irish Family History Research,* FFHS, 2nd edition, 1999.

Davis, Bill, *An Introduction to Irish Research,* FFHS, 2nd edition, 1994.

Erikson, Amy Louise, *Women and Property in Early Modern England,* Routledge, 1993 (Chapters 9 and 10 relating to widows and wills).

Gandy, Michael, *Basic Facts About Tracing your Catholic Ancestry in England,* FFHS, 1998.

Gandy, Michael, *Basic Facts About English Nonconformity for Family Historians,* FFHS, 1998.

Gibbens, Lilian, *An Introduction to Church Registers,* FFHS, 1994.

Gibson, J.S.W., *Bishops' Transcripts and Marriage Licences, Bonds and Allegations,* FFHS, 4th edition, 1997.

Gibson, J.S.W., *Probate Jurisdictions: Where to look for Wills,* FFHS, 4th edition, 1997.

Gibson, J.S.W. with Pamela Peskett, *Record Offices: How to Find Them,* FFHS, 8th edition, 1998.

Gibson, J.S.W. with C. Rogers and C. Webb, *Poor Law Union Records, Part 1: South-East England and East Anglia,* FFHS.

Gibson, J.S.W. with C. Rogers, *Poor Law Union Records, Part 2: The Midlands and Northern England. Part 3: South-West England, The Marches and Wales,* FFHS, 1993.

Gibson, J.S.W. with C. Rogers, *Coroners' Records in England and Wales,* FFHS, 2nd edition, 1997.

Gibson, J.S.W. with Elizabeth Hampson, *Specialist Indexes for Family Historians,* FFHS, 1998.

Grenham, John, *Tracing your Irish Ancestors,* Gill and Macmillan, 1992.

Guildhall Library, *Research Guide 6: Nonconformist, Roman Catholic, and Jewish Burial Ground Registers,* 2nd edition, 1993.

Harding, Vanessa, 'And one more may be there; the location of Burials in Early Modern London', *London Journal,* Vol. 14, No. 2, 1989.

Heal, Ambrose, *London Tradesmen's Cards of the Eighteenth Century,* Batsford, London, 1925.

Heal, Ambrose, *Sign Boards of Old London Shops,* Batsford, London, 1957.

Humphery-Smith, Cecil, *Atlas and Index of Parish Registers,* Phillimore, 2nd edition, 1995.

Joyce, Paul, *A Guide to Abney Park Cemetery,* Abney Park Cemetery Trust, 2nd edition, 1994.

Kaner, Simon, 'Mass Graves: Visby and East Smithfield', in Bahn, Paul G. (ed.) *Tombs, Graves and Mummies. Fifty Discoveries in World Archaeology,* Weidenfeld and Nicolson, London, 1996.

Leitch, David, '16th and 17th Century Breconshire MIs', *Cronicl* (Powys FHS), 34, April 95.

Leary, W., *My Ancestors were Methodists: How Can I Find out more about Them?,* Society of Genealogists, 2nd edition, 1990.

Litten, Julian, *The English Way of Death. The Common Funeral since 1450,* Robert Hale, 1991.

Litton, Pauline M., 'Dade Registers', *Family Tree Magazine,* July 1995.

May, Trevor, *The Victorian Undertaker,* Shire Publications, 1996.

Milligan E.H. and M.J. Thomas, *My Ancestors were Quakers: How can I Find out more about Them?,* Society of Genealogists, 2nd edition, 1999.

Mitchell, B., *A Guide to Irish Churches and Graveyards,* Baltimore, 1990.

Mondy, Isobel, *My Ancestors were Jewish,* Society of Genealogists, 2nd edition, 1995.

Moulton, Joy Wade, *Genealogical Resources in English Repositories,* Hampton House, Columbus, Ohio, 1988.

Moulton, Joy Wade, *Supplement to Genealogical Resources in English Repositories,* 1992.

Newington-Irving, Nicholas, *Will Indexes and other Probate Material in the Library of the Society of Genealogists,* Society of Genealogists, 1996.

Porter, Stephen, 'Death and Burial in Seventeenth Century Oxford', *Oxfordshire Local History,* Vol. I, 1980, pp. 2—7

Porter, Stephen, 'Death and Burial in a London Parish: St Mary Woolnoth 1653—99', *London Journal,* Vol. 8, No. 1, 1982.

Richardson, Ruth, *Death, Dissection and the Destitute,* Routledge and Kegan Paul, 1988; Penguin 1989.

Rugg, Julie, Researching early-nineteenth century cemeteries: sources and methods, *The Local Historian,* Vol. 28, No. 3, August 1998. This paper concentrates on sources outside Londonwhich may be available in local history libraries. It is illustrated with examples from towns and cities throughout England, Wales and Scotland.

Ruston, A, *My Ancestors were English Presbyterians/Unitarians: How Can I Find out more about Them?,* Society of Genealogists, 1993.

Schurer, Keven and Tom Arkell, *Surveying the People. The Interpretation and Use of Document Sources for the Study of Population in the later Seventeenth Century,* Leopard's Head Press, 1992.

Tate, W.E., *The Parish Chest,* Cambridge University Press, 1st edition, 1946; reprinted 1983 by Phillimore.

Wolfston, P.S., in Clifford Webb (ed.), *Greater London Cemeteries and Crematoria,* Society of Genealogists, 3rd edition, 1994.

Wood, Tom, *An Introduction to Civil Registration,* FFHS, 1994.

Wright, Geoffrey N., *Discovering Epitaphs,* Shire Publications, 1994.

Journals

Journal of the Association for the Preservation of the Memorials of the Dead in Ireland, Vols. 2—10, Dublin, 1892—1920.

The Local Historian, contains many useful articles.